SAFE IN THE ARMS OF LIFE

Edited by

Andrew Head

First published in Great Britain in 1998 by
POETRY NOW
1-2 Wainman Road, Woodston,
Peterborough, PE2 7BU
Telephone (01733) 230746
Fax (01733) 230751

All Rights Reserved

Copyright Contributors 1998

HB ISBN 0 75430 513 9
SB ISBN 0 75430 514 7

FOREWORD

Although we are a nation of poetry writers we are accused of not reading poetry and not buying poetry books: after many years of listening to the incessant gripes of poetry publishers, I can only assume that the books they publish, in general, are books that most people do not want to read.

Poetry should not be obscure, introverted, and as cryptic as a crossword puzzle: it is the poet's duty to reach out and embrace the world.

The world owes the poet nothing and we should not be expected to dig and delve into a rambling discourse searching for some inner meaning.

The reason we write poetry (and almost all of us do) is because we want to communicate: an ideal; an idea; or a specific feeling. Poetry is as essential in communication, as a letter; a radio; a telephone, and the main criteria for selecting the poems in this anthology is very simple: they communicate.

As Mary holds baby Jesus in her arms, we each cradle someone close who needs our help from time to time.

Safe In The Arms Of Life, is a collection of poetry based around the world of carers and the cared for.

Each poem shows just how hard it is to care for someone 24 hours a day, never switching off and always being there.

These poems are a dedication to all the carers and cared for; they give people a chance to let others know what their lives entail; the dedication, the hard work that goes into looking after another person and the effect it has on each of their worlds.

This anthology is a very poignant reminder to those people who dedicate their lives to helping and understanding the needs of others.

CONTENTS

Who Will Nurse The Nurse	Poppy Meredith	1
Relative Values	Peggy J Cornelius	2
Role Change	Rosetta Stone	3
Each Day	Ivan Sanders	4
Carers Caring	Dawn Maureen Kingsbury	5
And Where Am I?	Elizabeth Watts	6
Concern For The Carer	Jean Rendell	7
My Friend	Kay Gilbert	8
Waiting To Die	Sarah Ann Rees	9
Please . . .	Sue Garnett	10
Those We Care	Hilary Jill Robson	11
Someone Will Care	D Angood	12
Who Cares? We Care	Dolly Harmer	13
Vicki	D G Morgan	14
My Carer	Jenny Campling	15
Unsung Heroes	Julie McKenzie	16
Times Of Change	June F Allum	17
A Carer's Story	Joan Smith	18
Thanks Aneurin . . .	Donald J Butcher	20
Caring	Daphne Brooke	21
Fifty Years Of Glory	Kenneth Mood	22
Home Helps	C J Lewis	23
The National Health Service 1948-1998	G W Skaife	24
The National Health Service . . .	Katie Kent	26
Sweet Nurse	Michael Shimmin	27
NHS Hospitals And Carers	Jean P McGovern	28
Those Were The Days	Rose Thew	29
Post-Polio Syndrome	J D Bailey	30
NHS	Phyllis Bowen	31
Fifty Years - Who Cares?	R L Cooper	32
Custard	Alex Kennard	33
The National Health . . .	Don Goodwin	34
In Trust	Nick Colton	35

Praise To The Health Service	Wendy Watkin	36
The Operation - Ode To A Mr!	Mollie D Earl	37
Love	Winifred Brasenell	38
Granny	T Webster	39
Doctor! Doctor!	Kevin Murphy	40
A Private Ward!	Joan Scher	41
Well Looked After	Susan Mullinger	42
Untitled	Dorothy M Howell	43
Bed-Blockers	B C Watts	44
Samuel . . .	L T Coleman	46
Outpatients	Brian H Gent	47
Ballad	Linda Anne Landers	48
A Message On The Bed-Head	Peter Mallon	49
Casualty Clearing Station (1998)	Patricia McDonald	50
Things Have Changed	J Ellaby	51
Then, Now And In The Future	Eileen Simpson	52
Angel Of Night	D Yewdall	54
Operation - Healthcare	Paul Gold	55
Before The Pennies	Jacquie L Smith	56
Live In Hope	Eric Dang	57
Just A Cleaner?	Jill Bramhall	58
The Witch?	Valerie Thompson	59
A Mother And Her Daughter	Pauline Mary Tarbatt	60
Andy	Richard Monaghan	61
The Visit	Kit Pawson	62
Involvement Of A Carer	Bernice McCallion	63
Sweet Sorrow	John Wynn	64
Full Circle	Rosylee Bennett	65
Family And Friends	Mike Millard	66
Care For A Friend	Thomas Barker	67
Weary	Rowshownara Miah	68
The Alzheimer's Carer	Jill Parish	69

Dogsbody	Evelyn Balmain	70
Caring	Barbara Jones	71
My Mary	Penni Nicholson	72
A Caring Soul	Donna Distin	73
Star Shine	Anne R Cooper	74
I Do Not Want To Grow Old	Carole Bloomfield	76
For Childminders Everywhere . . .	Julie Hanstock	77
The Carer	Margaret Dorothy Davis	78
Nursing	Saiqa Mirza	79
Walking In The Rain	Maire Smith	80
The National Health Service	Jean Paisley	81
This Life	J Facchini	82
Angel	Michael Bellerby	83
The Carer	Pat Watson	84
Then And Now	Vivian Hayward	85
Hospital Appointment	Peter Comaish	86
Care	Clive Cutter	87
Creating A Monster	Amanda Richards	88
Untitled	Diana Stevenson	89
Battle-Axe	Lynda Sumbler	90

WHO WILL NURSE THE NURSE

Who will nurse the nurse
Now that she is old and frail
Trembling hands and face so pale
Who will nurse the nurse?

She sits all day, alone, in pain
And waits for a human voice in vain
Dreams of times that will not come again
Who will nurse the nurse?

In her youth she spent her years
Giving comfort, drying tears,
Allaying patients' bitter fears
Now, who will nurse the nurse?

She held new babies as they drew first breath
Stayed with the dying on the brink of death
Knew a mother's joy and families bereft
But who will nurse the nurse?

Her duties were heavy, weary from toil
Home based or on foreign war-torn soil
To her profession always loyal,
Will someone nurse the nurse?

Long gone her parents and her brother
Scattered her children, dead her lover,
And there has never been another
So who will nurse the nurse?

But now she finds a deeper love
As her spirit soars above
Rising like a peaceful dove
God will nurse the nurse!

Poppy Meredith

RELATIVE VALUES

When I was young and innocent and didn't know a lot
I wondered who the person was who lived with Great Aunt Dot.
She seemed to be a mixture, it meant no sense to me
The way she was depicted when the family came to tea.

Grandma said 'She is a saint.' Grandad said 'She's mad!'
Aunt Polly murmured 'It's a shame,' and Uncle Jack 'It's sad,
She's got the devil of a job, I can't imagine worse
She trained to be a teacher, not a twenty four hour nurse.'

The more I heard, the more it seemed a puzzling mystery
If she was mad, then how on earth, a teacher could she be?
A saint would wear a halo standing out around her head
But if it was the devil's job, would there be horns instead?

One day, when I was listening, another name was used -
'She's a geriatric carer' whispered Jane - I was confused.
She must be very special if she is called a *carer*
But Mummy said, 'Of course not, dear -
    It's just your Auntie Sarah!'

Peggy J Cornelius

ROLE CHANGE

The house was her kingdom
The kitchen her domain
But how things have changed!

Now he's the one who does
Every duty, all

The cup of tea on the bedside
Table, he made

The fashioning and styling of her hair
He combed, combed

The starched, clean sheets the machine
Washed, he ironed

The vacuuming, dusting and polishing he does
And with pride

To get in and out of her clothes, to give a helping hand
He is there

The shopping, a task he had always thought easy
Monumental

Terrorised! He gets her in and out of the bath
His face relieved

Nothing seemed different, everything the same,
House ship-shaped

Ordered! Only difference, he is
In her role

The house is now his palace
The kitchen his domain
And she, his devoted duty

Rosetta Stone

EACH DAY

Each day as I watch you die a little,
I die a little too.

Each day as I watch you cry a little,
My heart cries with you.

Each day as I see you stumble and fall,
I'm there to pick you up.

Each day as I watch you changing worlds,
I want to hold you back.

Each day as I watch you say 'Goodnight,'
I fear it will be your last.

Ivan Sanders

CARERS CARING

You gave your warmth and tender heart
To all you came in contact with
A smile a touch your presence it was not a myth
You took time to understand how you could help
Even the untrusting heart you could melt
You loved life so very much indeed
Caring for those who were so in need
Princess Diana was your name
You will be remembered always the same
A caring loving human being
Always in our thoughts never ceasing.

Dawn Maureen Kingsbury

AND WHERE AM I?
(Lines written after two strokes disrupted our lives)

I must be here if anywhere
Seated alone and waiting
Waiting for the *me* that I know
To arrive and take over . . .

These hours are my own if anyone's
A respite they say from caring
Caring for another that I know
Who has changed and taken over

> I hear a voice from somewhere
> Faint in its mournful complaining
> Struggling for some rhythm and form -
> Is it verse taking over?
>
> But verse of itself will not help me
> Seated alone and waiting
> Waiting for the me that knows *me*
> To arrive and take over

These hours which are mine if anyone's . . .
Drifting alone and still musing
Musing on the me that once was
And is lost . . . too soon over!

I must be here if anywhere
Seated alone and listening
Listening for the one I once knew
To arrive and take over.

> He is here (and not happily elsewhere)
> He is standing outside and waiting
> Waiting for the care I must give him
> To arrive . . . and take over . . .

And where am I?

Elizabeth Watts

CONCERN FOR THE CARER

Dear friend, I am so worried about you,
as I feel the hours you have to relax are really too few.
Burdened down with the care of others,
when something needs to be done it's dumped on you
by your brothers.

Work all day,
laughter stays away.
Money's short so he does not eat the food he needs,
and his dietary requirements he does not heed.
Because he sees he has no other choice,
the laughter is going out of his voice.
His face is starting to look so worn,
I long to help him and feel so torn.

At this rate you will be old before your time,
and rapidly go into your decline.
So take a deep breath and say,
today is for me I am going to rest and play,
before my time does come to cart me away.

Jean Rendell

MY FRIEND

In sickness and in health she vowed,
For better or for worse.
And now her husband's had a stroke
She has become his nurse.

For ten long years she's cared for him,
And never once complains,
But does her duty cheerfully
And helps to ease his pains.

She copes with gardening and the house,
Although she's nearly eighty.
I know of others too who bear
This burden which is weighty.

In this world where we daily hear
Of those who do not care
For any but themselves, these shine
Lighting the darkness everywhere.

Those who care and practise love,
Give hope for man's condition,
That he may turn from lust and greed
With true, heartfelt contrition.

Kay Gilbert

WAITING TO DIE

He's tired and weepy,
Restless but sleepy,
Family seeking,
Your help is needed.

Watching and waiting,
Half joking, half praying,
Jobs uncompleted,
Words for the keeping.

Confiding and hiding,
Feelings subsiding,
Consoling and folding,
The years have been moulded.

Waiting to die,
The clock is still ticking,
It's time to say goodbye now,
His heart has stopped beating.

Sarah Ann Rees

PLEASE...

Don't let me live to become demented
Alone in a world where my mind is tormented,
When my husband is dead, but I don't understand
And still look for the loving touch of his hand.
My children don't want me, or I wouldn't be here
Out of sight, out of mind, that's perfectly clear.
See my house full of strangers, I'm not having that!
I just want my own fireside, my armchair, my cat.
So please don't allow me to live on and on
When my husband, my home . . . and my mind . . . are long gone.

Sue Garnett

THOSE WE CARE

Remember those we have to care
Are on potent drugs,
To kill pain and bugs
Which give mood swings we have to share
With those we care.

They shout and scream and sometimes swear
But it is all bluff,
They are in a huff,
Frustration is what makes them flare
But they still care.

It's better to say a quiet prayer
To Lord God above
For those we love
When they feel life is so unfair,
We're there to care.

Times, days improve with those we care,
Maybe forever
With some endeavour,
Were life reversed we'd be nowhere
Without those we care.

Hilary Jill Robson

SOMEONE WILL CARE

Who will listen to me
when I grow old
and youth has gone.

Who will visit me
when in my room
all alone I sit.

When that time comes
as one day I know
it surely must

I will not despair
someone will come to care.
For in my God I trust.

D Angood

WHO CARES? WE CARE

I was a carer
I enjoyed my job
He was my spouse

When still a child
I dreamed of wedded bliss
And then we met

When we were young
Together we explored
The world around

When children came
Together we enjoyed
Our parenthood

Next we coped
With many teenage trials
As best we could

Enjoyed good times
In our middle years
Together grafted

When illness came
The quality of life
Was with us still

Now I remember
The joys of being there
I was his carer

And still he's there
I do not walk alone
He is my carer.

Dolly Harmer

VICKI
(Dedicated to all the nurses in the Royal Gwent Hospital)

When I first came into this world
Yes a little baby bouncing girl.
You weren't forced to be!
But who was there?
You were there to care for me.

As I grew day by day
Tall enough to run and play
To fall and graze my knee
Who was there?
You were there to care for me.

When I went into parenthood
You took me to one side, and I understood
What a good mother should be.
Yes who was there?
You were there to care for me.

Now I have come full circle
Old, frail I cannot see
Who is there.
Well you're still there to care for me.

D G Morgan

My Carer

Every morning, a little tap
A smiling face, a welcome
Along she comes, a smile
And gentle ways to share
It matters to me such a lot
That there are people who care
Without her smile the day is long
Sitting alone in my chair
These girls are called home carers
To me much more than that
Especially when the night is long
I share it with my cat
I know she will be coming here
Early, before it is light
Shining through my darkness
Making things look bright
Sharing, caring in God's name
I could not ask for more
And, I know that He has sent her
To come knocking on my door
To help me start another day
To cope with pain and sorrow
She shows me that tomorrow
Is just another day
Encouragement and kindness
That is her way
Because I know that she believes
As I believe, in God
I am sure her little footsteps
Step the way our Lord has trod.

Jenny Campling

UNSUNG HEROES

>Here is to the unsung heroes
>but they did not go to war,
>Who are brave and full of courage
>but have never waged war!

They are simple people like you and me
who have dedicated their lives,
To serving and helping others
every day of their lives!

>They work tirelessly tending to
>their loved ones day and night,
>And even though the task is daunting
>they continue in their fight.

There is no memorial built to recognise these carers
only our gratefulness to preserve their memory,
And the love shed abroad in our hearts
which will last an eternity!

Julie McKenzie

TIMES OF CHANGE

It was so very many moons ago,
I did nurse training, to people I'd show.
The sick, their burden, I'd try to share,
Proving to them, how much I care.
The aged the infirm, I'd help to the table,
Help them to feed, if they were unable.
Bedpans and bottles, I'd wash in the sluice,
Soak soiled linen, mop up spilt juice.

The work was hard, the money poor,
Job satisfaction, who could ask more.
Sitting beside someone, who lies very ill,
Praying and telling, God loves them still.
Today, hospital life has seen many changes,
New methods, and high technology ranges.
Shortage of staff, bring ward closures - no beds,
This is a plight everyone dreads.
Looking back over the years, I thank God above,
I had more time to care, being told 'Thank you my love.'

We have to move with the times, or so it is said,
In the past, more time to listen, and pray before bed.
How great, if time would allow, more worries to share,
So nurses today could give, more tender loving care.
Although under pressure, they all do their best,
Their love and their caring, ahead of the rest.
In spite of the changes, so many still moan,
Looking at the past, people, sigh and groan.
Perhaps, far from perfect, this, I do not jest,
Our nurses and carers, really are the best.

June F Allum

A Carer's Story

Have you ever been a carer
        It's not an easy task,
Looking after a loved one
        And doing all they ask.

I have been a carer,
        I know what it entails,
Alert from morning to night-time
        With a love that never fails.

Life is so very difficult
        Not like it used to be.
There's nurses coming in daily
        A big help to you and to me.

The doctor has to be called in,
        You are not very well.
A blood transfusion is needed
        As far as the doctor can tell.

Hospitalisation is the answer,
        The ambulance will be here soon
A bag has to be packed very quickly
        We have to be there by noon.

Settled at last in a hospital ward,
        It's time for me to go home.
There's washing to do, and a meal to be cooked,
        It feels very strange to be home alone.

The time simply flies, with visits each day,
        No time to relax and rest.
You're home once again and looking quite well,
        The treatment has been of the best.

How many times will this happen?
>I've counted twenty two times in twenty one months.
Until that January day, you slipped quietly away,
>Now my caring for you, is done.

Joan Smith

THANKS ANEURIN . . .

Ambulance here . . .
disabled, chair-bound handed aboard,
greeting fellow-travellers' levelling eyes.

Hospital . . .
disembark, seated, slotted,
progress reports to caring staff,
bantering jests with fellow-patients,
faint ripples lapping upon shores of silence -
whisked off to therapeutic apparatus,
working appetite for diet luncheon,
dextrously devoured by some,
others balk at bullet brussels.
Post prandial slumber, relaxation,
precedes session contortive flexions -
interspersed with widow's ululations,
feeling feathered touch of angel's wings -
kind George holds her hand.
Valedictory tea, attendance ends.

Ambulance home . . .
so here we are.
So what?
So let's recall with gratitude
Welsh wizard Aneurin Bevan,
all at-sharp-end H S workers -
ambulance persons, anaesthetists, auxiliaries, carers, chiropodists,
cleaners, doctors, nurses, paramedics, porters, surgeons, therapists -
the whole team,
A to Z.

Donald J Butcher

CARING

'Tis true, for some it's just a job
    They're paid to do - no more -
But most just choose to care and heed
    The cries they can't ignore.

Some travel far, may risk their lives,
    While many have to stay:
A card, a call, a hug, some flowers
    Show love a simple way.

The young princess who clasps a child
    Diseased and starved, and unaware;
The saintly soul who stoops to dress
    A beggar's sores - they care.

In sun-scorched lands, where peasants toil
    While water-holes drain dry,
Deep wells are dug and clinics built
    By those who hear the cry.

The carer with the listening ear,
    Quick smile, well-chosen joke,
Brings love and hope to helpless ones
    Cast off by other folk.

A child beloved, but handicapped,
    Needs Mum non-stop to care;
An unsung heroine, just like
    The other mums who're 'always there'.

The caring Christ, our pattern still,
    Shed sunshine in black night;
His touch brought health, His words gave life,
    His death - eternal light.

Daphne Brooke

Fifty Years Of Glory

Tony Blair loves the NHS
He wants to see it fly,
To be the best in the world,
Like an eagle in the sky.

Tony Blair wants to keep his promise,
To cut waiting lists,
To see us all smiling,
And making the nation more caring.

Tony Blair is our hero,
And he's got a difficult job,
Three cheers to doctors and nurses,
They too, have a difficult job.

Kenneth Mood

HOME HELPS

They make the beds
And scrub the floor
And many more things
Than they're paid for
During their morning round
Arriving as a friend
So many acts of kindness
With their work they blend.
Maybe they do the shopping
Or over a cup of tea
Listen to others' troubles
With genuine sympathy.
And while they wash the dishes
May tell a tale or two
Enjoying the daily gossip
As much as old folk do.
And sometimes during illness
Returning after hours
Or remembering someone's birthday
Gladden their day with flowers.
These 'dedicated daughters'
Working with a smile
Make many old and lonely folk
Feel life is still worthwhile.
'Home helps' are what we call them
Though in many grateful eyes
Not just the daily cleaners
But angels in disguise.

C J Lewis

THE NATIONAL HEALTH SERVICE 1948-1998

Congratulations to you all
In the caring NHS.
For your total devotion to duty
Treating patients in distress

It hardly seems like fifty years
Since nineteen forty eight
When we received free medical care
As part of the Welfare State

On a visit to the opticians
Or even the dentist's chair
Your every need was catered for
Free prescriptions everywhere

Life was frustrating on the wards
With equipment so old and worn
And nursing was so arduous
When the NHS was born

Though still the envy of the world
Despite trials and tribulations
Shortage of beds and waiting lists
And delays in operations

With the aid of modern science
Medical care is now so technical
By the skilful use of computers
Nursing today is so professional

You surely are a special breed
With your care and kind solicitude
For your fifty years of loyalty
We should all remember with gratitude

So I salute you one and all
Doctors nurses and paramedics
And all the other ancillary staff
As you tend your daily clinics.

May the NHS march proudly on
For another fifty years
Tending to our every need
And calming all our fears.

G W Skaife

THE NATIONAL HEALTH SERVICE - A MONUMENTAL MIRACLE

The NHS: a comprehensive medical service
Came into being in 1948,
Now it's 1998 and her historic 50th anniversary
We wish her many happy returns.
She had her trials, tribulations and criticisms
On her long lonely climb
Up the health service ladder.
She carried on cool and resolute
Seeing to man's killer diseases,
Enjoying rewarding recovery results
Leaving patients feeling assured and comfortable.
Lest we forget, the NHS stands for one and all
Setting in motion a good social climate.
Its priorities: healing, compassion and caring,
The river of life: doctors, nurses and domestic staff
Keep the NHS the best in health care.
The NHS had a beginning, but has no end,
Nye Bevan and co (1945-51) were its architects,
To those great departed men and women
It now stands as a dignified health monument.
May they rest in peace.
God bless and keep the NHS alive and well.

Katie Kent

SWEET NURSE

Sweet nurse come look upon me
I lie by fate undone
You bind my wounds so neatly
My gratitude you've won

And through the day you bring your tray
To bathe my fevered brow
Around the ward you work so hard
And smile for me somehow

Sweet nurse you look so care-worn
As night draws on its cloak
Your smile speaks now of sadness
What tale does that invoke

I hear you cry for those who die
And mourn for what is lost
You've eased their pain but all in vain
They've paid a bitter cost

Sweet nurse you've done your duty
I know the price you pay
Think now of all the good things
You do from day to day

Michael Shimmin

NHS Hospitals And Carers

When fracturing and breaking an ankle, I was carried away
Of course to a hospital, for a two week stay
While waiting a long time to see a doctor
People were screaming out with pain, I can well remember

Whatever has happened to NHS hospitals today
Why close them down for demolishing, and the ruins taken away
Where there was shortage of staff, one ward was left empty
It does not make sense, for the priority

When my leg was in plaster, and rising to the ceiling
Just makes us wonder how the short staff are so caring
They just could not do enough to help the patients
Guaranteed in all, nurses, carers had so much patience

When taken for X-rays, by good humoured porters
Many people were waiting, for the same treatment for hours
It never came as a shock, when they told the sad story
All through the lack of hospitals, closing as we now see,

When, arriving back home, there were carers indeed
Though underpaid, they worked hard, with such care that was in need
Making sure for safety, that no more accidents could take place
They gave so much help, through their caring moving pace

Thank God for carers, who are such a good blessing
And of course, for the doctors, through their knowledge of healing
Carers, doctors, nurses, work till they are tired out
Why should they be overworked, and underpaid no doubt

Most of all, I thank God for His strength to help me through
When reaching out to the Lord God, where there was pain and
                                                    shock, too
Whenever we see carers who work hard with their low pay
We need to see improvement for their future, and coming days

Jean P McGovern

THOSE WERE THE DAYS

I used to work at Westcliffe
I worked for the NHS,
That was in the days before
It got into such a mess.

I went to live in Jersey
When I was fifty seven,
When I first arrived there
I thought I was in heaven.

The year was nineteen seventy four
I was working at The Limes,
I made a lot of friends there
We had some real good times.

Now I'm back in Stoke-on-Trent
And everything is fine,
Although I am much slower now
Well, I am nearly seventy nine.

Rose Thew

POST-POLIO SYNDROME

This syndrome has me in its evil grip,
Causing my energy levels to dip.
I fight it with ev'rything that I can,
But it's making me a much lesser man.
Many are suffering helplessly
From this post-Polio malady
And still there is no cure within sight
To take us away from our awful plight.

J D Bailey

NHS

I sat in the surgery with other folk
Coughing and sneezing and looking forlorn
The wait seemed endless and I got so bored
I looked at the ceiling I looked at the floor
I read all the notices on the wall
Please do not smoke
I don't smoke at all!
Have you had your flu injection?
That's what I came for
I looked in my handbag found a pen and a sweet
I chewed it slowly then looked at my feet
I watched other patients bored like me
We could all graduate in a depression degree
I almost forgot what I came here for
Oh yes! That injection to relieve my fear
I don't want a dose of flu this year
'Your turn next' said the nurse with a smile
Making the wait and the boredom worthwhile
And I left with knowledge the treatment was free
Good NHS for folks like me.

Phyllis Bowen

Fifty Years - Who Cares?

Fifty years of the NHS
And who is it really cares?
Governments who cut and squeeze
And ministers who at their ease
Claw half the staff's pay-rise back?
Or a public who sing occasional praise
But don't give a damn about the shrunken raise
And the health workers' families' needs?
No! It's the doctors, nurses, cooks and cleaners
From all around the world:

The Fungs, the Yongs, the Shahs, the Keis,
The Tariqs and the Patels,
The Nandays, Petris, Fitaks, Habiebs,
Bansoodebs and Bridgelals,
The Kalwas, Flunges, Tymoszczuks,
The Sreeharis and the Sampus,
The Okrafos, Cayabyabs and the Singhs
The Mungars and the Vasimus,
The O'Loughlins and Mackenzies,
The Wigmarajahs and Chrysostimous.

And there's many one with an English name
Who came here from lands abroad,
Developed, developing and Commonwealth.
They came and cared and stayed,
Stopping tears, allaying fears,
Comforting and supporting;
How strange it is to call National
What is so internationally served.
How strange it is so unappreciated
Except for weasel words.

R L Cooper

Custard

Tick tock:
Time passes away the lonely hours,
A nurse pushing a trolley
Has a ladder in her stocking,
The patient watches the trolley
And the nurse washes the patient,
Soap suds flowing over naked chest
While she thinks of coffee and the shopping list
And custard.

The surgeon stands tall.
He is for:
Directness? Breakthrough and the knife.
The patient hears:
Sorry we took both eyes out,
Cut off your ears and
Blocked up your nose with
Wax.
Whilst the doctor says:
Yes? Fine, good: Out tomorrow.

The nurse's ladder grows longer
And the patient attacks the
Dinner,
But the dinner fights back
And wins.

It is dark? Darker? Black outside,
And favourite television shows are on,
Bring back memories of home
And take away those of tomorrow.
The patient is awake to sleeping pills and:
Lights out, it's time.
Time for what, the . . .
No: just time for bed.

Alex Kennard

THE NATIONAL HEALTH...

The National Health Service has gone to pot,
No one's happy with their lot.
When mistakes are made they're covered up quick,
The secrecy really does make me sick.
It's bad enough seeing things go wrong,
Want not to bite my tongue.
But my job will be at stake,
If the muck around I rake.
My real name I cannot say,
I want to work for another day.
If I were to disclose my real name,
They would deny it just the same.
Politicians don't really give a toss,
They're in cahoots with my boss.
He doesn't use the hospital at all,
A private consultant he does call.
For his wife and kids he does pay,
If he used my hospital they'd change their ways.

Don Goodwin

IN TRUST

There was a young man named Kinnock
Shouting: Oh! Flipping 'eck.
They're demoralising the nurses
And pinching their purses.
It's the NHS they're trying to wreck!

Nick Colton

PRAISE TO THE HEALTH SERVICE

With much responsibility and round the clock care,
Thank you to the Health Service,
We're glad you're there.
We've come a long way since bygone days,
Things have changed a great deal.
So much for the better,
I'm sure you'll feel.

Many diseases can be treated, easier than long ago,
But to find a cure for everything,
We've a fair way to go.
We have to admire the surgeons
With their dedicated skills,
Often working throughout the night
To cure people's ills.

Busy doctors work long hours,
Nurses do their share.
Easing the suffering of the terminally ill,
Many a tear.
Caring for the elderly is never easy,
But with patience things get done.
Emptying bedpans, cleaning wounds,
Not a lot of fun.

From surgeons to ward maids,
Our lives are in their hands.
They do their best to comfort,
To help and understand.
So how would life be?
Think what you would miss!
There'd certainly be a difference
Without a *Health Service.*

Wendy Watkin

THE OPERATION - ODE TO A MR!

On a bright day in June she first met this Mister.
One look at her tum made him sigh then - 'Oh Sister.'
So - beguiled, when he smiled she agreed to his terms
When he promised to rid her of all of them germs.
For she came all a'tremble a'feared and a'fright
Never guessing she'd find such a gallant 'white' Knight.
'There's nothing to fear - you're here in our care
One week with us here and you'll be walking on air!'
With a grin and a laugh he bemuses, bewitches -
The next thing she knows he's got her in stitches!
'I'm cut up about it' she told him next day
I don't mind the Dr but what about Mr Fay.
Oh Mr Fay what a Toby you are
If I'd known what was coming I'd been back in the car!
So deftly was done all the cutting and splicing -
Not quite sure who did all this 'feather-stitch' icing!
Her fate's with them all the Doctors and Nurses
Take no notice of moans, her groans and her curses
She's really enjoyed the company she's in
To have missed it would surely be a 'cardinal sin'!
As she struggles to stand with an 'oh' and an 'aah'
And finds that she really cannot go that great far;
As for doing the splits it's really not on -
She might try a bit later when 'stitches' are gone.
As fit as a fiddle she surely will be
Once she gets over this little lark and a spree.
So although it's OK and she knows he's 'au fait'
'Fraid come what may - it's 'Goodbye' to Fay.
'Many thanks for your skill your kindness and care
This Mundesley Moll will remember you there!'

Mollie D Earl

LOVE

Carers are sent from heaven above,
With so much patience caring and love,
Angels from heaven they play their part,
Reaching out to others deep from their heart.

Whatever their daily task they do,
With kindness, smiles and compassion too,
Tenderly caring for those in despair,
Showing how they really care.

We thank the Lord from heaven above;
For these dear carers who share their love.
To others in need with every care,
Making their lives so much easier to bear.

We'll pray and ask the Lord to bless
In every corner of this world
For those who bring such happiness
With their hearts of gold.

Winifred Brasenell

GRANNY

I cannot grieve
already she is a shadow
in that great light
she came to us in love
delicate thread of light
strung tight within her;
beside her always stood
her dark angel.
Waiting, at last she
turned, gave herself to him -
all that secret pain
encompassed her being
she is gone but happy.
No, we must not grieve
but love her, remember her
forever

T Webster

DOCTOR! DOCTOR!

Can Doctor Brown keep the temperature down?
After all he's the new doctor in town
I wonder what he hides beneath his gown?
I wonder what he hides beneath his frown?
Is there something the matter with me?
Come now doctor can't you see?
I know your advice isn't free
I wonder what fills you with glee?
I wonder why you are so nice?
Are you now thinking of the price?
With NHS cuts it's now twice
The normal and coming up for thrice!

Kevin Murphy

A Private Ward!

Should I have a private ward with BUPA?
The NHS will help they say
But not a private ward, oh no
Into a general ward I go,
And I might have to share with men.
Then if that's so,
Out of bed, that's me, and home I go.

Why should I have to share with men
But then . . .
I'm in my seventies, stiff and grey
But so are they
Well so they say . . .
They wouldn't put *young* men in too,
But if they do
I'll stay . . .

Joan Scher

WELL LOOKED AFTER

Without a National Health Service, I think where would I be,
I'm grateful to all the local staff, for looking after me.
A frequent patient, I've always received wonderful treatment,
When in an emergency, to the hospital I've been sent.
Nurses, calm and confident, reassure me with ready grins,
Even diagnosing consultants, have smiles, which are welcoming
There are many volunteers, who help out as hospital guides,
They serve cups of tea, perform other menial tasks besides.
Porters push trolleys and wheelchairs, often whistling in full song,
Make my stays in hospital bearable and not appear too long.

Susan Mullinger

UNTITLED

What can I say about the NHS
They are good to me, I must confess
I could not wish for better care
When I'm in need they are always there
In casualty or surgery, I've been in both of late
And never had a long time to wait
My doctors always explained what is wrong with me
And maybe in a year's time I will not see
But I have faith in NHS, they'll do what is right
To remove my cataracts and give me back my sight.

Dorothy M Howell

BED-BLOCKERS

The school years are over,
Teenage plans are not to be
For now the war has started
And no future can we see.

The guns are loudly booming,
The planes are overhead,
We have an indoor shelter,
It is our usual bed.

All the food is rationed
And our clothing too,
If it wasn't for our make and mend
I don't know what we'd do.

But now the war is over
The 'boys' have all come home,
They've had their fill of travelling
No more they wish to roam.

They settle to the daily grind
Don't ask too much from life,
They simply find contentment
With a family and a wife.

There was a simple promise
The government then gave,
We would be taken care of
From the cradle to the grave.

But care is not for everyone
For we have now been told
That we are just 'bed-blockers',
No use, we're getting old.

Hitler thought the same way
And I would like to know
Now they've started on us oldies
Who will be the next to go.

B C Watts

SAMUEL -
A NATIONAL HEALTH SERVICE NURSING AUXILIARY

Samuel, comes from Ghana,
A massive, gentle, man,
Tall, upright in every measure,
With magnificent elan.

He takes his duties seriously,
And always gives his best,
Ensuring that his services
Will always stand the test.

He works for many hours, in shifts,
And walks for miles and miles,
In lifts, on corridors and stairs,
His broad face wreathed in smiles

To patients, he is courteous,
With simple style and grace,
The normal honest dignity,
Belonging to his race.

If ever you're in hospital
And feeling rather low
You'll need a friend, like Samuel,
No matter where you go.

L T Coleman

OUTPATIENTS

The Waiting Room is full today
As staff and patients interplay,
A hearing aid, an eyesight test,
The staff will always do their best.

All therapeutics here designed,
By specialists of every kind;
I'm sitting next to Mr Clegg
Who has sustained a broken leg.

Mrs Wilson's daughter Rose
Has got a pea stuck up her nose,
Then there's little Jimmy Tucket
With his head stuck in a bucket.

Mr Smith, who is very stout,
Is having trouble with his gout;
Across the passage, Mr Brown,
Must have the largest boil in town.

So thank you to our NHS,
Is just the point I'd like to stress,
The way that since, I don't know when,
All we need is an FP 10!

Another thing, beyond description,
(Available without prescription)
Is all the friendships that prevail
Through treatment for my ingrown nail!

Brian H Gent

BALLAD

We're moving Nearer Heaven Slowly,
Where the spirit is non-divisive
and it is second nature to heal and be healed.

We're moving Nearer Heaven Slowly,
where the once was quality of life
will be our last remaining thought.

We're moving Nearer Heaven Slowly,
taking with us the hell or heaven
of the human condition,
where death is immaterial
yet war and pain are still wept over.

We're moving Nearer Heaven Slowly,
So don't you try to rush us,
among you devils Angels are still walking,
so grant us some good luck.

We're moving Nearer Heaven Slowly,
but which of you will join us?
Here everyone's in spirit,
everyone's a healer, there's no waiting,
and healing is its own reward
and no one earns a packet.

Linda Anne Landers

A Message On The Bed-Head

An old man stricken,
imprisoned in a hospital bed,
by the crime of disease.

The tubes and machines,
that surround his tired body,
like a deathly breeze,
blows air into his fire,
louder than he breathes,
yet they remain his only friends,
supplied by the NHS.

And here I stand before him,
full of youth and life,
can walk away at any time,
and I feel his eyes,
piercing into my heart,
judging my youth a crime,
his body screaming to me,
'take all you can from life,
for no change is given,
in the currency of time'

Peter Mallon

CASUALTY CLEARING STATION (1998)

Don't leave me in this corridor,
Frightened and all alone,
Waiting for an x-ray.
A veteran from a home,
Lying here on a trolley
I'm in pain constantly,
Barely dressed, and this thin blanket
Hardly covers me.
Six hours wait, and yet still
They pass me right by.
Perhaps next time they come along
My plight will catch their eye.
Old, unattractive and unloved
A statistic with no family.
I'm NHS - no hope for some -
A forgotten casualty.

Patricia McDonald

THINGS HAVE CHANGED

Where is the Matron, no more they said.
So who to complain to from my sterile bed?
Who plumps my pillows when nurses are busy?
Who answers my buzzer when I'm feeling dizzy?

Where are the doctors so grey and mature,
Now they're so young and exhausted for sure.
Bring back the old days, the starch and the rules,
Fair deals for nurses don't treat them like fools.

Why are the visitors here all the day?
When I want to sleep they just get in the way.
Never a vase for the flowers they bring,
No one to answer the phone's urgent ring.

When I get better perhaps I should stay
And roll up my sleeves, if I'm not in the way.
Maybe I'd cope in the long dreary night,
Or maybe the hassle would give me a fright.

How do they cope when they're worn off their feet,
With only the odd box of chocs for a treat.
Why should I moan when it all comes for free,
So patient be 'patient' exactly like me.

J Ellaby

THEN, NOW AND IN THE FUTURE

The National Health Service,
Where would we be without it?
But - read the history of health:
In the 1930's, when people died from lack of treatment
All that was needed then was wealth.

Twice in a lifetime the NHS
Has been there for me when needed
(But one must be watchful - think of dentistry!),
I was the recipient of differing care,
But trust was placed in the surgeon's skill.

The noble vision thing was there in 1957
When the NHS was squeaky clean and really caring,
No internal markets then
And money not the first consideration.

The dreaded operation was postponed a week,
Allowed to stay through bronchial problem,
Never mind, they said, it will be done next week,
Meantime stay and have a rest,
In preparation for the operation.

Hard to imagine in 1987
How humane the NHS was in 1957.
In 1987 time and money were the paramount concerns.
A major operation; my trust in the surgeon's skill rewarded,
But aftercare left much to be desired:
Shortage of nurses, dirty corners, awful meals,
And they said in a few days you will be leaving.

Why a month's stay in 1957 and a few days in 1987?
Oh, they said, with modern medicine you'll be fine,
You are behind the times; anybody at home to help?
One had to accept but it's not exactly seventh heaven!

No, health can't be gained on the cheap,
I don't know the answer but
Good health was the criteria for all,
And we must pay according to our means.

Long live the NHS, so hardly fought for by our peers,
Go forward, retain the best,
But take lessons from yesteryear.
Remember Bevan and the vision thing.

Eileen Simpson

ANGEL OF NIGHT

As I lie on my bed of pain she appears
So I know ere long she will dry my tears.
She may not appear to have gossamer wings
Wear a halo or play on harp strings
But to me, with these tired old eyes of mine
She looks like a guardian angel divine.
As the dread dark hours of night unfold
She's a shining vision to behold
As she ministers to 'wants' the whole night through
Giving kindly attention and comfort too
As with soothing hand and gentle word
Night Sister patrols her geriatric ward -
And as sleep evades me she's by my side
And listens as I pour out my thoughts like the tide:
As I tell of my childhood and the games we played
The clothes we wore (often home-made)
I've not always had this crippled old frame,
I have lived and loved and kindled a flame,
Then my wedding day when I took his name.
How we survived war with its blitzes and bombing
When he was sent aboard we wrote letters of longing.
Then of our reunion with joy and laughter
The birth of our children, a son and a daughter.
But, the love of my life died a year ago
So I tell her - 'Now I am ready to go
To join him wherever he might be
And can't wait now my love to see.'
So she takes my hand this Angel of Night
And leads me gently towards the Light.

D Yewdall

OPERATION - HEALTHCARE

In 1948 - the Labour Government introduced the NHS
Which was financed, in weekly contributions, by the working class,
Hence - no more outlay - for visiting your local doctor
Or - for operations, by the maestro behind the surgical mask.

For the past 50 years, thousands of citizens have had operations
Without the worry of 'Can I afford?'
Plus - the tender aftercare - by our wonderful nurses
It's become almost a joy - to lie in the ward.

Yes - the health service has proved a boon and a blessing
The 'man in the street' is now living, to a ripe old age,
Past sixty - past seventy - past eighty,
Some, in the nineties, are still turning over a new page.

However - this longevity has put a great strain, on the medical world
Your local GP - has little time to rest - night and day,
Waiting lists for hospital beds - have become horrendous
Many better-off patients, have decided to go private - and pay.

Our present Government is pledged, to cut hospital waiting lists
If you are at the back of the queue, you may still hum a song,
Whether it's hip replacement - heart attack - or hernia
With a little patience - it should not be too long.

Many foreign countries - envy our National Health Service
Our care in hospitals - plus food and drink, and a warm bed,
Today - the Health Service may not be 100% perfect
But - don't take my word
Have a chat - with those resuscitated from the dead.

Paul Gold

BEFORE THE PENNIES

We were sick, before they came, of everything
that gave us pain, it was the cost that pained us
most. A decade's gestation, only five survived
uncertainty of early years. No anxiety pills to calm
the fears, that grave tomorrow claimed.

In life and death we lived with our dis-ease
like it was a friend, who had no bedside manner
but stayed until the end. The bedridden years
we never thought, as odd, we coped in hardship
as best we could.

We didn't claim our rights, our wants, but lived in hope
of better days. Bevan's pennies saved our lives. And now?
It seems they fight and strive, for everyone, must stay alive,
no one may die, no one grow old, or put up with
a common cold! Pain-free existence, the eternal goal.

Was this what he worked for, in bringing millions
free health? Was this the vision that he saw?
Where we now spend our lives complaining
that we never have enough, and this painless life
we search for, still, dependant upon wealth?

Jacquie L Smith

LIVE IN HOPE

All the anguish, all the pain,
living from day to day,
kept alive by a kidney machine,
the wonder of modern day.

Three times a week on dialysis,
four, five or six hours a time,
one boring routine,
like a car production line.

Can't eat or drink what I like,
most foods are taboo,
for if I dared break the rules,
I'd be dicing with death, that's true.

All I can do is live in hope,
of a near-normal life again,
is that one day in the not so far off future,
a transplant comes along,
so that I can be reborn again,
well and fit and strong.

Eric Dang

JUST A CLEANER?

She left home late this morning, rushing for work once more,
scooped up a bag of wool, grabbed keys and then slammed the door.
Clean white tabard pressed and folded, high pinned-up long hair,
to another day, cleaning, clearing up and doing a fair share.

Undoing things, doing up things, helping all who come her way,
sometimes smiles, sometimes a tear, because it is all in her day.
A smile she takes as her thanks, from the receiver of the wool,
a nice lady, now not very mobile, but she is nobody's fool.

In the next room is a lady, who is kind with a smile all day,
once a famous published poet, but poor health got in the way.
Every person has a tale, they are from all walks of life,
some have been lucky had life easy, some have had their strife.

Next door the man still is sleeping, she goes to tell the carer,
who nods saying it is the long sleep, she wishes life was fairer.
Then on to a gentleman, who well, does not want to be in care,
he may blame this young girl, because, he has to have her there.

Finding false teeth in strange places, because of failing sight,
listening to stories and hoping that all the answers are right.
All have interesting adventures of their past, so much to tell,
now all look to this young lady to help and to answer their bell.

She comes as just a cleaner, and the cleaning just goes on,
but will also fetch library books, or shopping as she goes along.
Just one of the team of the many staff who are there to care,
and all are sad to see someone gone, each heart has a share.

Cleaners, care assistants, a hairdresser all have a part to play,
and several other roles take place to help along life's way.
Then there is the chef who mans the stove and serves the fuel,
but matron has the final say, so that no one breaks the rule!

Jil Bramhall

THE WITCH?

We were all alone with you, you sat in the chair
you spoke with a croak, and we had such a scare.
Hair long and straggly, your nose seemed so long,
we dared not move a muscle, we tried to be strong.

We thought you were a witch come to cast a bad spell
to change us into frogs, or put us down a well.
But after a while, we found you were just old
and here to take care of us, we then felt less cold.

You only had two teeth left, so what did we do?
We gave you some chewing gum, to see if you could chew.
But you sang us some songs to send us to sleep.
Memories of our baby-sitter! our treasures to keep.

Valerie Thompson

A Mother And Her Daughter

I watch them chatter,
A mother and her daughter having tea
Around them teacups clatter
They're so happy in each other's company.

Her child's food lovingly cut into pieces,
A napkin laid beneath her chin
A gentle hand smoothes out the creases
To allow her feeding to begin.

So careful not to spill a drop
The food consumed and now she stops
Mops up the dribbles around her chin
The task complete, more battles yet to win.

She takes her child's arm tenderly
Helps her totter to her chair
Sits her down unsteadily
Strokes and smoothes her daughter's hair.

An everyday picture of a mother and daughter
One that we witness every day
Except the child is a woman, her chair a wheelchair
Her mother, her carer still, in every way.

Pauline Mary Tarbatt

Andy

I met her in the swimming baths
As I swam up and down,
Thrashing about in my rubber ring
Trying my best not to drown.
I'll never forget our very first date,
Apart from the fact that she turned up late!
For instead of remarking about my wheelchair,
She was more concerned with the state of my hair!
'You're bald,' she said, 'that's odd for one so young,
I thought you said you were twenty-one?'

'Did I say that?' said I, thinking quick,
'Well, I've had a hard life and I've been quite sick.
Maybe thirty-two is more the mark,
But that doesn't mean I came out of the Ark.
I still have the urge for romance you will find
Even if most of it's now in the mind.
So let's have a cuddle, tickle and slap,
Before the nurse calls for my afternoon nap!'

Richard Monaghan

THE VISIT

Frail fingers
fret and twitch the rug marked
-*Ward 9 Men* -
Nurse folds about your chair.

Grieving
I watch the mindless movement
of those hands,
age stained now
yet strangely soft and childlike:
the hands
that plucked my innocence
made me wise.

I reach out
and clasp your fingers:
you gaze
at me
through me
past me.

Nurse tells me
you are happy in your world:
it is only I
who rage
at the nothingness in your soul.

I urge you to feel
pain, anger, passion:
instead
you smile -
benign
serene
so bloody indifferent.

Kit Pawson

INVOLVEMENT OF A CARER

Caring is demanding,
There are many roles a carer has to play.
The complexities of life packed into every day.
A motherly resident is passing away
The carer has to be brave and stay.

Life was slowly ebbing from my kindred mother
Fully alert and wide awake she gave so little bother.
Content with all the little things
My hand upon her brow
'How good it feels,' she kindly said
Could we only do it now.
If she would only stay alive
Oh! How selfish human nature
To do our best to keep her from a much more peaceful future.
Her kindness flashed before our eyes
We knew, but feared to think
Those welcoming arms would soon be cold.
'Twould only take a blink.
So precious is life and yet it goes so quickly.
We held her living person there
But the hand that held her hand
Was slowly made aware.

Bernice McCallion

Sweet Sorrow

Swinging doors and the doctors on call
Nurses' station just along the hall
Distant motion as alarm bells ring
With relief comes a pointed steal sting
Masks and tubes abound
Rhythmic comfort from the monitors sound
Graphs and flickering lights of green and red
Grouped and hovering just above the bed
Visiting time and all is well
Smiling faces and stories to tell
Chocolates, cards, flowers and sweets
Caring hands bearing eats
Recovery steady but painfully slow
Progress made and eager to show
Discharge pleaded and sort in vain
Frustration mounts in anger and pain
Shifts change with beds to make
Trembling limbs raise and smiles fake
Daily rounds, and inspections made
With salutations and compliments paid
Days come and weeks pass by
Tears of joy you can now cry
Such sweet sorrow
Hasten the dying night and come tomorrow.

John Wynn

FULL CIRCLE
*(Dedicated to the memory of my beloved Father,
Eric Lowe, 1918-1989)*

*Once you cradled me, held me tight
Tucked me in before saying goodnight
Once you sung me this lullaby
'Hush, hush my little one, don't you cry'.*

The roles have reversed with the passing of years
Now it's I, who is doing the wiping of tears;
It is I, who comes running whenever you call
It is I, who is picking you up when you fall.
Now it's me getting up in the middle of night,
To chase troubled dreams and to hold you tight.
No longer the child, but a woman full-grown
Returning the love through the years you have shown.

It was you who taught me the right way from wrong
Who clothed me, and fed me, so I could grow strong.
A more faithful parent just did not exist
For my welfare was always the top of your list.
'One who taught me, in all things I needed to learn,
Your life's turned full circle, and now it's my turn'.

It is me who is now helping you up to bed
It is me who takes care you're well cared for and fed
Who is washing and dressing and keeping you warm
It is me making sure you're kept safe from all harm.
'My Father, dear Father it's ironic somehow
That life's turned full circle, and it's *my* turn now'.

Rosylee Bennett

FAMILY AND FRIENDS

Now I have the measure of what they gave me,
One parent gone, the other creaking towards the millennium,
Day by day a little less able
To do the simple things I take for granted
Like opening a jar of marmalade.

What great stoics they are, these wartime people,
These doodlebug survivors from another age,
This dwindling band of make-do-and-menders,
Put out not so much by their rusting joints
As by the sheer mad speed of things these days.

Now I have the measure of what they gave me,
One parent gone, how shall I honour the one remaining
Now that her old familiar world has gone to seed?
Her family fragmented, her wartime friends
Hanging on in seaside towns.

Now the honeysuckle is in bloom
And with this scented summer breeze comes an image
Of the place I'd like to take her,
To a future rich in people and events
Where family and friends are close at hand,
Never quite perfect but still better than of now.
As it was before, when she was but a girl,
A single town or village to contain them all.

Mike Millard

CARE FOR A FRIEND

Do we help, when we hear a baby cry
do we ask the reason why
are they lost, or are they sad
a tummy pain, or just feeling bad

Can we help someone with pains
give them shelter, when it rains
or do we turn the other way
and close our ears, to what they say

Can we sympathise, and share their grief
do we rob them of their belief
In their greatest hour of need
can we not do a friendly deed

If illness strikes, will we stand
or do we lend a helping hand
do we show them kindness and give them aid
and expect their gratitude to be repaid

Unselfish attitudes do we show
assistance and help wherever we go
will we help to the bitter end
what more can we do to help a friend

Thomas Barker

WEARY

She rocked me as I cried,
soothing me with gentle words,
murmured in my ear,
I fought down the pain,
the urge to lash out,
because of this stranger,
I was forced to remember,
remember the mother who never cared,
who never loved me,
or hugged me,
but this woman hugged me,
like she cared,
and so I cried,
cried until there were no more tears left to weep,
and yet the nurse held my shaking body,
until I rested my weary head on her shoulder,
and slept.

Rowshownara Miah

The Alzheimer's Carer

He sits in his armchair, alone in the room
Thinking his thoughts, feels only despair and gloom.
How did it happen? Where did she go?
The woman he married, who once loved him so.

He cooks and he cleans, he does his best
Yet some days he longs for a leisurely rest.
But he married his lady for better or worse
So he's chief cook and bottle washer, her own private nurse.

He gives her a bath and washes her hair,
She only looks past him, she's not really there.
But oh! How it hurts when out of the blue
She looks straight at him and asks 'Who are you?'

Fifty years they've been together as husband and wife
He cannot imagine her not in his life,
And she seems happy in her own befuddled way
Whilst he just gets lonelier and sadder each day.

Jill Parish

DOGSBODY

Underpaid and overworked
That's the nursing staff.
Cheerful to the nth degree
To them a toast I quaff.

'I'm sorry nurse, I need the loo,'
Or else, 'I have no water.'
'There's something wrong with this machine,
Not doing what it oughter.'

Blood pressure, pulse and temperature,
Coffee, Horlicks, milk or tea,
Make the beds, tote that chair,
How busy can you be?

Hurrying here, chasing there,
Why did I choose this vocation?
I'm the one who needs the care,
The most tired in creation!

Dayshift, nightshift,
Weekends are the same,
Whew! I think I'm really tired . . .
'But nurse, I'm glad you came!'

Evelyn Balmain

CARING

He started to fall and his legs would give way,
We would laugh as I helped him to stand,
But the numbness was worsening, and unsafe to drive,
Retirement came earlier than planned.

We were hopeful at first, but the doctors were blunt,
'There's no treatment, just do what you can.'
I saw in his eyes that the willpower had gone
And the long, lonely fight had begun.

We battled together and coped for a while,
But the struggle was too much to bear;
I watched in dismay as he slowly withdrew
From a world that he deemed so unfair.

The stiff limbs grew stiffer, mobility gone,
Now he needed my care day and night,
His brain still so active, his body so weak,
He was locked in a cell without light.

I prayed he would talk to me, give me a glimpse
Of the hell he was feeling inside:
I washed him and dressed him and tended him still,
But deep down in my heart something died.

Guilt plagues me - I feel that I failed in some way
To console him before his life's end;
But he suffers no more, he's at peace with his Lord,
And I loved him, my husband and friend.

Barbara Jones

My Mary

She struggles out of bed each night,
To take me to the loo.
She washes me, and wipes me.
The things she has to do!
And when I say, 'Oh thank you dear,'
She smiles, and says, 'Love you.'

I know like me she's getting old,
And spends her life in pain.
Yet she does so much for me,
And never does complain.
And when I say, 'Oh thank you dear,'
Her smile shuts out the rain.

My Mary cares for me each day
I am a lucky man
Because for love she serves me well,
In every way she can,
And when I say, 'Oh thank you dear,'
She smiles and says, 'Oh Dan!'

When at last God takes me home,
I'll whisper in His ear,
'Don't leave my Mary all alone,
Bring her to me, up here.'
And when I tell my Mary this,
She smiles and sheds a tear.

Penni Nicolson

A Caring Soul

Every day she lives for others
In her work and private life
Whether working with the elderly
Or as a mother and a wife
She's befriended many pensioners
On their loneliest last years
And when they're let in Heaven's door
She's shed a good few tears
It's more than just a job to her
Not only shopping and house cleaning
Sometimes they only need a friend
That's what gives her job such meaning
Her caring ways are full-time
Not just when she's out at work
For then she tends her family
Who I'm sure drive her berserk
Always there to help them
She'll give more than she'll take
Her devotion to her family
She never will forsake
To the elderly a saviour
A friend who's like no other
To me she is a martyr
My kind and caring mother.

Donna Distin

STAR SHINE

The heart of a caring person you'll really know
Because the love from them you'll feel just flow
It won't be just charm or surface show
They will speak to you and won't tell you to go
How many times have we been shown rebuff
From the very folk we thought had love
Yes we're made aware we're imposing on their time
And to ask for a minute seems a crime
It's not that you're demanding or attention seeking
It's a human need for another human-being you're needing
This world has a lot of toys, cars, tellies, a lot of noise
But they are not flesh and blood, they can't give human love
Even an animal can let you know that your presence is needed so
No it doesn't want the remote control, it wants your heart and soul
In places that would shock you to the bone
People are left sitting all alone
In some hospitals people look around
And there is not a soul-mate to be found
The medics just do their job and are forever writing notes
Very seldom do they ever relate to us folk
And we wonder how some people just lose the will to live
Maybe it's because we just did not give
This money-rush materialistic world will always be here
But remember your neighbours are very very dear
Yes our eyes are sighing very forlorn
As we quietly register all that is wrong
We look up to the person that demands status
But when we're gone can that person replace us
Well I have to say I've experienced all this
That is why the caring person is just bliss
All day passed and everybody rushed about harassed
Then Nan the night-nurse sauntered in
And you'd thought she'd discovered her next of kin

The sun shone from her face as over to my corner she smiled amazed
Well, I had felt like something the cat dragged in
But Nan you made me realise my heart could sing
So what do you say this poem is all about
It's the caring people we want to shout and tell you all about.

Anne R Cooper

I Do Not Want To Grow Old

It's so very sad when you grow old
and your home and possessions are all sold.
They put you in places so that you are not alone
where overworked carers do nothing but moan.
They are so busy, they don't have the time
to care for us properly, it's such a crime.
They also have to keep the place clean
but this is not possible and the smell is obscene.
Stale urine lingers wherever you go
our unwashed bodies make us feel so low.
Some of us wander all through the night
we know it's not day, but can't get it right.
Day or night it all seems the same
some of us cannot even remember our name.
Why do they make us live here like this
it's not what we want, something is amiss.
My mind is still active but my body is slow
I wish I could leave but have nowhere to go.
If only they had more time for a talk
or even to take me for a little walk.
I would like to be with people like me
not surrounded by others full of senility.
I feel sorry, the workers do what they can
but are thwarted by policies which belong down the pan.
They work so hard for little pay
but no-one will listen to what they say.

Carole Bloomfield

FOR CHILDMINDERS EVERYWHERE - UNSUNG HEROES OF THE PRE-SCHOOL WORLD

We care for all the little ones,
Another mother's daughters, sons,
We smile through all the tears and joys,
Of other mothers' girls and boys.

We're there to love them when they're sad,
We're there to counsel when they're bad
To hug and comfort when there's pain
And splash through puddles in the rain.

We greet them with a warm 'Hello!'
But, feel as happy when they go!
To put one's feet up, a cup of tea,
Then in comes hubby 'What's for me?'

Julie Hanstock

THE CARER

The child within me cries
Silently as the grave
Wherein my Mother lies

No more happy laughter
Only tears
Longing for the arms
That enfolded me over the years

In times of trouble
Times of strife
Always there throughout my life

Mother's problems kept out of sight
A carer was she
That was her plight

When the big *C* came
No-one saw beyond the depression
That she bore - so bravely

Planning a holiday to cheer her up
'Devon' she said, with a sad smile
Her request was simple
So much pluck

On the last day her hand traced my face
'I do love you,' she said
And died with quiet grace

Margaret Dorothy Davis

NURSING

I could not rid myself
    Of the hatred
      I held
      I housed
      I harboured
      Inside of me
    Sometimes it was weak
    Sometimes it became stronger
    Once I was able to maintain control
      Now it was uncontrollable
    I had nursed my hatred so much so
      I was the one that was becoming damaged.

Saiqa Mirza

WALKING IN THE RAIN

Two young girls in the park
heads close together, talk earnestly,
walk, heedless of the rain,
under dripping trees, try to comprehend,
ease all that wild bewilderment of pain.

All in the mind. Take the nerve-tonic, find
plenty to do; be determined, be strong.
Only your own willpower can pull you through;
the remedy . . . a half-century ago.

In a crammed Bedlam, years
of imprisoned youth pass; drinking tea together;
behind the silence, fears,
a world I cannot enter.

Through convulsive therapy, leucotomy,
searching for words to say
'Mammy won't come again.'

Prime of life and changes come; afternoons out,
cream teas, learning to smile again,
weekends home, then here to stay, first holiday,
independence and your own place

We've had our ups and downs, despair,
laughter after defeat; we meet,
we part, each holding her secret hurt;
frontiers still uncrossed between we two,
but one thing I know for sure, that being free
is what means most to you.

Then I recall the way it all began
and ask myself . . . why you, not I,
remembering two young sisters, walking
in the rain, in the park.

Maire Smith

THE NATIONAL HEALTH SERVICE

Aneurin Bevan piloted this bill through in the past.
The British National Health Service was really meant to last.

In times gone by the poor could die even without a pill,
they could not buy a medicine every time they were ill.

Our working-class had painful deaths and childbirth was a lottery,
both going out and coming in was full of filth and butchery.

But, now we have a Bayer Company saving us from pain,
it's time the National Health Service was using them again.

Just now the poor in Britain get drugs so weak and slow,
only the Service shutting down could be a bigger blow.

Even in the olden days drugs were not in two classes,
the strong stuff for the very rich the rubbish for the masses.

Lots of things just can't be done this can be understood,
but, make things fair across the board what we get should be good.

Jean Paisley

THIS LIFE

A baby comes into the world
In hospital cot lies warmly curled
Health visitor comes because she knows
The things to watch for as he grows.
School clinics too for various needs
Safely through the growing years leads
Then on to families of their own
All care supplied for as they've grown
Hospital, GP all are free
Physically and mentally.
Old age comes, frailty increases
Eventually to death releases.
All through this life there's been a wealth
Of service from the National Health.

J Facchini

ANGEL

You are my angel bathed in soft light
Attending my needs through the dark of the night
Nothing it seems is too much for you
A smile from your face gives me fresh hope anew
This is your world we only see a small part
And these words that I write are straight from the heart
Is that without your dedication and professional charm
We wouldn't be so relaxed, peaceful or calm
To return to our families all safe and sound
Knowing there's someone you're now watching who's glad
                                         you're around

Michael Bellerby

THE CARER

He did not even know her,
This woman in his home.
She never ever left him,
He could not be alone.
Where did she come from?
Who gave her leave to stay?
He yelled and screamed and taunted her -
She would not go away.

She did not seem to know him
This man she loved so dear.
She knew she could not leave him,
She knew she must stay near.
The joys they shared together,
The vows they made to care,
Were lost to him forever
In suffering and despair.

They struggled in their misery,
They fought the endless fight.
To him she was a stranger;
To her he was her knight.
His dragon was bewilderment,
No memory of the past.
Her anguish was his agony,
His crying broke her heart.

Two souls lost in the wilderness of love and hate and pain.
Pray God the last analysis will make them one again.
He a loving husband; she a caring wife.
Please bring them back together in another, sweeter life.

Pat Watson

THEN AND NOW

For twenty years I worked for you
The good old NHS
With money short and hours long
We always did our best

It was instilled in all of us -
'The patient heads the list,
They're frightened, ill and vulnerable,
Care counts' - staff would insist

The NHS God bless them all,
They saved my husband's life.
Thanks to their care and supreme skill,
We are still man and wife.

The hospitals we knew and loved
Are now all known as 'Trusts'
A name let down by those in charge
Of money saving 'cuts'.

A business now, it seems to me,
Of auditors and such
With all the staff behind the scenes
Not mattering quite so much.

Why can we not amalgamate
Thinkings old and new
To give us back the NHS
We once so loved and knew.

Vivian Hayward

Hospital Appointment

I've struggled to the hospital to get my niggles checked,
to see if I'm just past my peak, or if my body's wrecked.
I'd make a brilliant waiter, yes, I've hung around so long
I could serve each ailing person in the world with egg foo yong!
Do they care for poorly patients, all these doctors with their 'phones
carried round to interrupt our unacknowledged gripes and groans?
Will they try to test our patience, will they try to make us think
that the fact we're here just illustrates we can't be in the pink?
Oh, the longer I'm imprisoned here, the more I'm getting fraught
so afraid potential ills will spoil my medical report.
Has my pulsing blood been curdled, or the X-ray shown up blurred?
Are my twanging nerves lethargic and tired arteries well furred?
At last my name is called: I carry on to hear the worst.
'Will I survive?' I manage, keen to show my feelings first.
'Relax, you're in great shape,' she says, 'We've found there's
                                            nothing wrong.'
I should be pleased I'm not diseased, but I'm sick it took so long!

Peter Comaish

Care

Care?
Oh yeah,
We all do, don't we,
A little tamely.

Try?
Oh my!
Of course we do, don't we,
A little lamely.

Succeed?
Yes, indeed.
The signs are obvious, aren't they?
Care? Oh yeah, as I say.

Clive Cutter

CREATING A MONSTER
(A celebration of fifty years of a National Health Service
Which is free and available to all)

Transforming sights into a vision,
Beautiful as the moon,
Frankenstein made his monster.
A weight of surgical, iodine flesh
Stitched into cumbersome shape.
Ugly and lost under critical, sterile lights,
And misunderstood.

Transporting rights across a people,
Romantic as a kiss,
The physician laid his healing,
Raising us from our animal howls.
Wisdom in a lunatic state.
There is no cost which can be measured against this gift
Of common good.

Amanda Richards

UNTITLED

Broken Bones -
In the orthopaedic ward

After the operation
I lay in a daze,
My legs were frozen

Later the consultant came.
Smiled kindly, felt my now moving toes.
Said, 'You'll be fine.'

The nurses were kind,
They eased my embarrassment of
Asking for the bedpan,
They helped me wash.

In four days, I was out of bed
And walking on crutches, and
Going home.

But
Behind me I left more
Broken bones.

Diana Stevenson

BATTLE-AXE

Carbolic smell,
        polished floor, every inch so clean;
starched sheets,
        aprons too, uniform pristine.

Steaming sluices,
        pungent ether, matron on her rounds,
barking orders,
        nurses quaking, efficiency abounds.

Sister watching,
        staff nurse clocking, every move she makes,
beady eye,
        all perusing as the errant nurse she shakes.

Sends her off
        to fix her cap and mend her tattered hose;
smart attire essential
        from her temple to her toes.

Discipline and order
        prerequisite for the task
to heal the sick
        and make them well, not a lot to ask.

Not one thing
        out of place, not one speck of dust,
no breeding ground
        for germs here, sterility a must.

Hygiene and obedience,
        alertness day and night;
the only way
        to run her show, the way to get it right.

Bully girl,
        tyrannical traits along the corridors,
marching on relentless
        like a starving lion she roars.

But rue the day
> she went away, her kind are now extinct,
and the lowering
> of standards, are maybe somehow linked.

So, battle-axe
> we need you back with all your dedication,
to save
> our ailing NHS and the health of our nation.

Lynda Sumbler

SUBMISSIONS INVITED
SOMETHING FOR EVERYONE

POETRY NOW '99 - Any subject, any style, any time.

WOMENSWORDS '99 - Strictly women, have your say the female way!

STRONGWORDS '99 - Warning! Age restriction, must be between 16-24, opinionated and have strong views. (Not for the faint-hearted)

All poems no longer than 30 lines.
Always welcome! No fee!
Cash Prizes to be won!

Mark your envelope (eg *Poetry Now*) *'99*
Send to:
Forward Press Ltd
1-2 Wainman Road, Woodston,
Peterborough, PE2 7BU

OVER £10,000 POETRY PRIZES TO BE WON!

Judging will take place in October 1998